Laws of Emotion

Thought Provoking, Heart Rending 100 Selected Poems

MOJIBUR RAHMAN

PUBLISH AMERICA

PublishAmerica
Baltimore

First printing

PublishAmerica has allowed this work to remain exactly as the author intended, verbatim, without editorial input.

Softcover 9781630043025
PUBLISHED BY PUBLISHAMERICA, LLLP
www.publishamerica.com
Baltimore

Printed in the United States of America

DEDICATION

First and foremost, I must dedicate this book to my wife and children without whom I couldn't have possibly accomplished and completed this book. Next, my heart felt dedication goes to all who strive to bring justice and fairness among the oppressed peoples of the world and to those who with their knowledge and hard work show them the true and right path to follow.

ACKNOWLEDGMENTS

My gratefulness and appreciation goes to Jill Beadon who with her great zeal and eagerness went through the contents of this book word-by-word and line-by-line not falling short of suggestions and alterations. At the same time I must not forget the other two worthy readers namely Rose Williams and Dorothy Winters for their ideas of emotional nature.

Table of Contents

Mad About You

What really makes me mad about you?
Well! It's really not easy for me to say.
There are myriad of things that you do.
Such as your wild passion at mid-day
changing into freezing droplets of dew.
Just to tease me, side-by-side you lay.

If I have to lose myself in your being.
And drown in tears to make you smile.
Even if your heart is unwilling to sing
the song that we sang for a long while.
How can I bear the sorrow of suffering?
In your love I'm like a lost floating isle.

Sanity is a boon but not without peace.
Hard it is to live with your wild desire.
A few more months or years on lease
and unrest shall burn in my heart's fire.
Sad I am to find that you are so at ease
yet restless I am to see you and admire.

Wish to love and be loved is my need.
So lets try to be wise and use our brain.
There must be a way to make you heed
to my wishes and think of loss and gain.
And above all you need my love to feed
your hunger of obsession never to drain.

My Belief

So many a times I stand face to face with my belief
and ask myself if I was to lay aside my basic need.
Would I still be a caring man or be like a winter leaf
destined to be shed as the trial of life begins to heed?

Belief guarded by wisdom and reason stands at ease
among an army of fickle and fussy devout wild souls.
How to win their hearts and minds before they cease
to live by the rules of reliance and conviction's calls?

Liberty and freedom is hyped in the name of masses.
But its outcome is often left for the future to decide.
Do I commend or condone their futile acts that lashes
at the ethics of those who adhere to the rules denied?

Where are those who aim to unfold unity and peace
without any facts and reasoning of belief and trust?
Would they know why I yearn for healing my heart?
Not before we are all ashes to ashes and dust to dust.

Love is to...
Forgive and Forget

I fail to cry when my heart aches.
Looking at me the gesture she makes.
It is her thoughts and carelessness
or possibly her concern, more or less.
Out of her way she intrudes into mine
by the cringe, I cannot forgive.
And there she goes again
asking me to forget.
How could I ignore from the very outset?
She always insists love is to forgive and forget.

Whether or not I am happy or in pain
it makes no difference to her.
As far as she is concerned
she holds a double-edged sword in her hand.
From the one edge, she slices my rising ego
with other, she makes me kneel.
One can imagine my state of affairs
and how I must feel.
A lady with her all heavenly assets
isn't truly willing to divulge all her facets.

Should I blame her for what she does?
It is in the nature of the beauty
to uphold and stand for the rarity of this gift.
Possession without any guilt or remorse of treaty,
vows of cordial nature to extend without any rift.
Accepted to be within her lifestyle
more or less when taken into account
all that goes through her mind all the while.
In reality she isn't cruel at all.
It's just the way she touches my soul.

Once in a while I plunge her in a state of disbelief.
From whence she is unable to emerge
that makes her impulsive and abrupt.
Out of place and distant she takes step to submerge
all her promises and vows.
The acts of this sort always create a rift
between the two souls meant to be one.
How to forgive when she is always in my heart?
And forget? Well it isn't as easy as it may seem.
I do really believe love is to forgive and forget.

No Ifs and Buts

Never to prolong this notion of quest
and never to argue in vain.
Never say no and leave your nest.
And no ifs and buts with a view to gain.

What if notion of quest is quashed
with set means or ways?
Or no conflicts and no row to settle.
Will there still be an emotional maze?

Surety stands to guard all deeds
frivolous or firm in nature.
And gates of loss or gain
remains locked within this feature.

A change of will or an urge is in need
to push insight to its brim.
Just there you will gather
the lost love light bright or dim.

Shape of a Man

Love sneaked into my life in the shape of a man.
Kind and caring with a tale of the days gone by.
Poured out all he had hidden in his broken heart
and got rid of the misery of being a lonely guy.

So gladly I greeted him with hope and happiness.
Only to find his sweet love has now turned sour.
In merely a few months of being heart and soul
his love became spiteful and mean within an hour.

How do I hold on to some one and who to believe?
This thought pierces my heart now night and day.
Is love truly hard to get and even harder to know?
And devotion out of reach and affection far away.

At times it's really hard to be a woman in love.
Relying fully on one man for his love and support.
Then again, I could have him like a hand in glove.
Or make him twist and turn deep in my thought.

Betrayal of Destiny

A soul, confined and caged within the body
with a vocation to uphold.
To remain faithful with the future concealed.
Betrayal of destiny, always to be ignored.

The burden of living with the fate unknown
and a treacherous path to tread?
Like unpalatable food ordered to digest
by unseen hands, forced to be fed.

What if honesty is always hard and testing?
No short cuts or easy way out.
Does the trial of life not end with loyalty?
Or the deeds fix the fate of devout.

Like the opposites such as good and bad.
Betrayal faces loyalty in all walks of life.
Whereas destiny is the result of our deeds.
Bonded, just like husband and wife.

Chasing Dreams

Wild and strange it may seem to others.
But my world of dream is as real as me.
In pursuit of love I have lost all my zeal.
Chasing dreams when awake, never to be.

How to follow the sight with closed eyes?
Even when sound is nowhere to be heard.
But my dreams have dived into darkness.
Unwilling and opposed to fly like a bird.

Control of longing is beyond my reach
and reality is there to behold as mirage.
The more I pull my out stretched arms
stronger is the urge to leave entourage.

Stand still or changing place to conquer.
Fears and worries are there for me to face.
Like a perceptive believer I stand at ease
with all my dreams, that's always the case.

Prized Punishment

From dawn to dusk I long for his embrace.
But the night brings its own grief and pain.
His grin cuts through me like a sharp mace.
Prized punishment to have, no love or gain.

There comes a time when his heartless love
dives in my care and regret returns to haunt.
Friendly feelings turn into a push and shove
and pretence gives way to a tease and taunt.

Love versus hate and desire against despise
the two ends are always there laying in wait.
How to choose between the truth and the lies
when I do not know the depiction of my fate?

Loved for life and guarded with utmost zeal
soul of my life is all set and ready to leave.
Though, heat of my passion he may not feel
in guilt and loss of love he's surely to believe.

Pleasure with Pain

At a loss, knowing not what to call this feeling?
I seek happiness but sorrow is there to greet me.
How to resolve this dilemma of double-dealing?
Pleasure with pain is always there to defeat me.
When sorrow faces happiness in my blissful life.
And when there's no more delights left to enjoy.
I find comfort in the arms of much reviled strife.
But there's a spot in my heart for her to occupy.

I mustn't let my anger to cast a shadow of doubt.
Even my feeling about her has turned to a craze.
Then again, she is looking for a reason to shout.
Although it may bring in her life an awful phase.
It seems she has made up her mind not to heed
to my undying plea of keeping peace and quiet.
So, there is one thing I must do to make her lead
the hedonistic life without fears and out of sight.

The Difference Between... Vanity and Pride

When vanity becomes the focal point in someone's life.
And pride occupies the seat at the peak of life's domain.
When conceit reaches the rank of glamour to beat strife.
The difference between vanity and pride drops like rain.

Could it be that a will to act sets a trait, an urge to lead?
This in turn reveals his or her cruel and callous conduct.
Disregard the needs and wants that causes harm indeed.
No regrets if others are kept aloof, with a will to abduct.

Humility cries when a soul is beaten with a moral slant.
Allow not, rules of a kind to imprint alien traits to bear.
Breaking codes of modesty turns even a friend to chant.
Slogans, turning to the ways that infuse subliminal fear.

Under the veil of vanity the failings of a being may hide.
Though time-to-time it reaches to a peak only to mourn.
Whereas pride seeks out the natural instinct only to abide
and capture lost and lonesome souls from dusk to dawn.

In Search of Bliss

I told her in earnest.
Something is missing
from our nest.
Please let's go let's go.
Looking at me in amazement
she shrugged her shoulder
and whispered.
Are you really my friend or a foe?
Holding her hand I replied.
Be quick or we'll miss
all the fun of love on the go.
Roaming around in search of bliss.

Together, I want to be
without any trail or track.
Just follow the echo of your heart.
There is no reason to look back
at the footprints we've left behind.
Let's hold our wishes in a rucksack.

Hidden in the corner of my heart
lies a forsaken glitter of hope.
Still waiting to lift
the misery of trail unable to cope.
Wasting moments gifted to us
by the tick of time, let's just elope.

Then again why bother to follow
the unseen fear?
The awful cry of befallen sorrow.
It isn't good for us my dear.
Leave the future where it lies.
At the ends of the Earth far or near.
An act of pretence or a show of passion
desirable it may seem to her.
But I quite disagree to sow the seeds
of discontent just to create a clamour.
My aim in life changes from one to another
bliss, pleasure, grief and gloom.

I know not when and how
to find and fulfil the emerging needs.
Destined to be a winner or a loser
try to meet all her wishes and desires.
My search for bliss will carry on
till my love finds harmony.

Destined to Lose

I try my best to keep her in line with my thoughts.
Though she fights and builds a barrier to our talks.
And then my fear joins with haves and have nots.
I'm destined to lose unless I watch her like hawks.

Courage it takes to bear the many tricks she plays.
Her ups and downs lead me to her favourite game.
How do I stand in step, out of step or in her ways?
It's becoming a life long task to confront in shame.

A plan of action and skills to impress her is need.
Ways of mixed gains should be brought into play.
At a point of no return, I must give her a new lead.
Before she says goodbye or simply wanders away.

Made by nature to bear the stress not just by name.
Change of fate is not for those who seem to reside
within the limits of self-denial to regain their fame.
I am forever yours, if you promise to be my bride.

Union of Our Hearts

Strangers we are but beyond words when our eyes meet.
The world ceases to be, while my breath stops and starts.
Longing of my heart grows to a height to raise my heat.
And with all my zeal, I wish for the union of our hearts.

You know we dwell upon the parallel means of living.
Though at times we may tell our secrets to one another.
Impossible it is to lead my life in this sort of misgiving.
We must resolve our differences and move a bit closer.

Fusion of soul, doesn't seem to be a ground to uphold
that we can stretch to meet the two ends of our feeling.
In view of the mess can we make this secret to unfold
the truth of the matter, then resolve it by wise dealing.

We differ in our thoughts but we are truly two of a kind.
And we do agree to disagree when we have to reconcile.
There are no secrets in our lives for the feelings to find
the union of our hearts still in the state of being so docile.

Tears in Her Eyes

In each and every corner of my heart
a mass of dead memory lies.
For so many years I have grown
aches and pains and seen its demise.
I can still drown in the onslaught
of heart rending tears in her eyes.

Time and again I ask myself.
Why did I have to vanish without a trace?
No clues, no signs and no love to show itself
and no cause to bring a smile on her face.
Must get back to the way we were
before the loss of old memories we share.

Gloom in my life ends with a spark of hope
and her heart beats with happy feelings.
Is there a challenge out there for me to cope?
No, there could never be any bargains or dealings.
How to evoke smiles on her face?
A quest is on night and day with all factors of interlace.

To soak away tears from her eyes
I have laid a table of resolve with love and peace.
All that is needed now to make her recognise
the safety of love for life and not on lease.
Above all she is mine as I am for her
for now in this world and thereafter.

Just a Sight of Her

There must be a reason for this restive feeling.
Pounding of heart beyond its vigour and drive.
My want for her looks is more than appealing.
Just a sight of her makes my heart come alive.

Why I feel tense when she asks me to go out?
I know she loves me but I still have my doubt.
My urge is strong as soon as she is in my sight.
And I fall prey to her wishes night after night.

Like an aura unseen though always around her.
Fixated to fall blindly in love under her charm.
A craze it seems to be from afar one to another.
It isn't meant to cause any hurt nor any harm.

I have laid all arms of defence facing her zeal.
Never to say no and by no means suffer or feel.
Under valued even if she snubs my entire plea.
There is no other soul so dear or lovable to me.

Kisses

Like the golden rising sun,
like the full moon.
Like the mid-summer's day,
in the month of June.
Like the new buds of the roses,
bursting to glow.
Like the kisses from your lips,
just restless to blow.

Parting of lips or just dying to close
unlike a lonely and unloved rose.
It can never hide
made up kisses or stolen pride.
But it can surely display
the glamour of the day.
With wisely chosen words
to head high or fall to decay.

Your awakening desire rest at ease
with me in my lap of praise.
Kisses, trying best to invoke its effect
upon my heart, set ablaze.
Neither you nor I have the control
upon its progress or outcome.
I always try to make you feel happy
without you I feel so lonesome.

Kisses to console, kisses to please,
kisses to love and kisses to appease.
Kisses on the forehead,
kisses on the lips and kisses on the cheek.
Kisses of the wedlock,
kisses of the birth so mild and meek.
Kisses at the occasions yet to be unveiled
and kisses in love most passionately hailed.

The Difference Between... Innocent and Naive

The difference between innocent and naive is
like the two sides of a coin.
Purity and chaste oozes from the one side
whereas on the other, youth and immaturity shine.

The confusion arises when sides change
and innocent is blamed to be naive.
Or naive is stigmatised to be innocent
till there is no other rationale to believe.

The phrase innocent till proven guilty
points to a testimony without any disbelief.
Whereas maturity is the key to unlock
the cage of adolescence setting it free.

Where to place innocent and naive
on the scale of difference?
There doesn't seem to be any parallel base
between the two misconceived words or phrase.

Love of My Life

Purity and innocence is the focus of her being
from the sleepy cradle to the apex of all strife.
An emblem of my life open to all for viewing.
She is a true gem and the only love of my life.

But she goes against all my views and wishes
and breaks all usual rules, vows and promises.
As she grows she learns to live by alien belief.
How do I swap this kind of shock with relief?

Whether or not my love will continue to grow
depends on the way she treads the path ahead.
She has to choose inviting or dull, high or low
from the dish of life without being spoon-fed.

Still she wouldn't let me down just to hurt me.
My love will show her the way to good deeds.
And even if she falters on her way then I'll be
so happy to guide her and fulfil all her needs.

Silent Words

Sparkling eyes, deeply laden with emotional longings
is more hypnotic than the songs of the tweeting birds.
Open or closed, either way it hides the wealth of love
and other feelings, untold, unspoken like silent words.

True it is that our wishes are caged inside the eyelids
and longing gets restless to spread the wings of zeal.
Wordless revolt rises to lift the veil of hidden passion
only to find a loving host of looks have stolen the feel.

Spoken words that rhyme with our innermost desires
but lacks the sense of belonging and refutes true needs.
False promises and vows that disgrace poise and hope
always stands to lose credence in life and good deeds.

Like the rain-seeded clouds, silent words do not rumble
but leave the long lasting mark in our hearts and minds.
Such is the outcome of virulent gaze oozing from eyes
with its silent words even enemies surrender and binds.

Close Your Eyes and See

The best way to gather the depth of feelings
is to open your heart and close your mind.
Even then, if you can not sense or take it all in
to glance even deeper close your eyes and see.

Gazing out banishes feelings of your heart.
Scorched eyes are no longer keen to see.
Yet, beyond the horizon of skirmish desires
there is no other way to save your senses.

With your open heart and closed eyes
you are bound to see your feelings aflame.
Burning inside and shiver out to a long freeze
a sigh of relief or a soothing heartthrob to blame.

Now is the time to relax, close your eyes and see
at the feelings at large out of control.
What is the outcome of this ongoing episode?
Storm of feelings inside and rumble of thoughts out.

Born to Lead

Like a star I shine at the seat of power.
Come what may I'll never go away
from doing my duty of the day.
Given this right by selection at sites
of the whole nation with adoration.
Who is to deny? It is I, who was born to lead.

But to be a leader, I do have to follow, their
wishes, wants and promises I made so hollow.
There could never be a compromise or deal
between my goal of life and what the others feel.
Party opposite trying to defame and overthrow
I declare all their efforts to be gobbledygook and low.

Nobody? I just couldn't be in this house of fame.
Though my weakness lay hidden within
troubled mass of souls and problems I may not resolve.
Trust bestowed upon me now seem to sway
under the stress and strain of the agenda of the day.
So, I mustn't allow my will to wane what I believe to be.

Destiny has guided me to the place where I feel at ease.
No doubt, I hold the key to the door of the house
where fates of the people are bought, sold or put on lease.
There is no reason why I should not excel and seal
the deeds of the day by virtue of being in majority.
And show what a hardheaded leader aught to be.

The Difference Between... Opinion and Verdict

Opinion stands to express our acquired views
or our thoughts about a number of issues or objects.
Whereas verdict is a decision arrived at or taken
in the light of proof and scrutiny of given subjects.
Above all, opinion is just an educated guess
and verdict, a conclusive result clear to show and depict.
At times resemblance between the two is clouded
as opposed to the difference between opinion and verdict.

Problem arises when opinion is taken as a verdict
even though it lacks a credible source.
On the other hand a verdict is undermined for being feeble
just because it has no eminent force.
Yet sometimes opinions are graded to be high or low
based upon the social repute of individuals.
No argument or point of view dispels its effect
and no legality is beyond the scope of its rituals.

Disbelief is there to throw any thoughts of the kind
which allows an opinion to get a foothold.
Strong or weak there is a spat of unease in the air
for the show down to be daring and bold.
Within the sphere of doubt but below ones estimation
there lies the seed of wisdom.
To endorse or turn down the said act of appraisal
becomes the means of a trial or welcome.

Opinion and verdict may stand side by side for the show
and there is no point to mix and match.
But there is a particular occasion when these two
misconceived and misused phrases could separately hatch.
Above all opinions do not hold any binding roots to adhere
to the grounds of acclaim and applause.
Whereas verdicts are the chain of legal force for the people
which keeps the unruly within the laws.

Middle of the Road

I realised at the midpoint of my life
that there was a crucial fact I have ignored.
I blindly followed a path that kept me aloof
of a way of life in the middle of the road.

A risky left or a dangerous and dodgy right
both sides always seemed to be full to the brim.
There were no beacons of truth to fight
the ignorance and hate miles away out of trim.

Then life isn't really straight and easy to live.
Though I have tried to live it in so many ways.
One way or other I just seem to swim around
in the murky waters of life for days and days.

After dawn and with every dusk of the day
I never seem to catch a real peace of mind.
Surely there is a hope for some one like me
on the middle of the road a heaven to find.

It was Never to Be

So near, yet beyond my reach, some one like you.
I had never thought I would share my life so soon.
One day, so graciously when you crossed my way.
Just like a new moon it was never to be at midday.

How to weave an emotional web to tie your heart?
I am already drawn to circle the events of your life.
Wherever you move, you won't keep me far apart.
Trouble is that I can't have you as my wedded wife.

I have tried hard to break out of your eternal hold.
But I am much nearer to you now than I used to be.
Perhaps you are waiting to behold my love unfold.
Yet it isn't the end of the beginning for you to see.

I must keep on wishing for the day of your return.
No wailing or cry of being the last one in the line.
My only regret is that it remains a one-sided burn
with a longing heart and lonesome feeling of mine.

Free to Choose

In the scheme of creation
first and foremost, we are gifted
with grey matters called brain.
No imposition and limitless desires
span of adventures absolute
and lifted to a height
full to the brim never to drain.
And free to choose our own empires.

The rules are there to guide
the scheme of events to consider.
Wishes and wants embroiled with needs
knocks at the door of freedom of choice.
Subdued and submerged within
the raft of living day-to-day.
Knowing not how to escape the confines
of living no more than once or twice.

Escape from dreams is not an easy task
distress and pain is there to greet.
Retreat or drown in the river of aspire
or be brave and run on your own two feet.
Dwell upon the thought of being
in a place no one has ever seen.
And imagination could never catch a glimpse
of a shape or size that has never been.

Caught in the web of words such as free
our sixth sense is deluded by desires.
Choices are only there to make us believe
that we have to escape into the depths of reality.
Though we can spread our wings in the air
and fly to choose countless goals.
Truth of the matter is there is no such thing as free
inside bodies we always find residing souls.

Dying for Peace

At the heart of chaos and conflict
there lies a deep distrust and disbelief.
There isn't a means or a way to reconcile
narrow mind and a heart so obese?
Then at the edge of the sphere of life
there are those who dare to create clamour.
They just cannot bear to see the souls alive
they are all at war just dying for peace.

Over the years oppressed living
has made all to walk away from reality.
Knowing not what path is right to tread
and how long to bleed their conscience.
Bodily wounds they are to endure
under the supreme rules of the time.
But they are unable to resolve daily issues
arising from the root of belief and obedience.

Facing a wall of oppression stands
an army of subjugated souls.
Weak but not beaten or defeated
yet keeping their goal of life in sight.
Striving to win not just for themselves
but through the war of wisdom for mankind.
Dealing with the ultimate challenge of death
pushing the frontiers of war day and night.

A mountain to climb or over the seven seas
there is no way to stop the waves of their zeal.
The only wish in their lives is to go forth
and conquer the land of peace and tranquillity.
They all stand shoulder to shoulder to sacrifice
their livelihood, family, friend, young and old.
Their only aim in life is to unearth peace
at any cost even at the expense of wilful death.

Truth is Hard to Believe

A fact that needs no support or proof for it to be.
Stays the same even when cast to vary in shape.
Domain or dialect has no impact upon its make.
Truth is hard to believe and even harder to fake.

When truth hides a clue of fictional nature to save
life of a downtrodden hiding for safety in a cave.
Like a face in the mirror distorted and misplaced
truth peeks into the eyes of reason so displaced.

Easy to say and easy to show is the way to lies.
Beyond doubt there are many ways to despise.
Truth becomes the subject of claim and debate
for the outcome in life such as destiny and fate.

As a rule approved matters entails no testimony.
Though at times it's hard to show its real worth.
Like the day that gulps the night but with agony.
Such is the charisma of truth right from its birth.

Accept Me the Way I am

Appalling and awful I may seem to you.
Then not every one is the same.
I try to show you my nature good or bad.
Accept me the way I am.

My honesty may seem harsh at times.
But I cannot betray your trust.
I will always come out straight.
No matter even if it seems to you unjust.

A change in my views towards you.
May bring a little comfort for a short while.
Then I wouldn't be there to take care.
And all my deeds will reflect as vile.

So let us agree to a norm of dealings.
I try not to intrude in your way.
If you agree to accept
my love and the way I show it day to day.

To Live My Life

Is there a way to flee from this daily clash?
And leave behind all this life of mishmash.
Get my blissful peace to slumber and sleep.
Move away to live my life silent and deep.

Strife in life is not any longer hard to bear.
But all the while I shake and shiver in fear.
Like the raindrops my needs wets my brain.
To wash away all my faults down the drain.

What if my fate is to be the slave of events?
And all my deeds turn into wailing laments.
There is no avenue to turn and no way out.
Just stay with the routine without any doubt.

Tranquil thoughts and patience is in need.
To weigh up my future and fortune indeed.
Step on the set path for the future in mind.
Make every effort for the comfort to find.

She was Right

She asked if I had an option to choose
between the day and night.
What would I choose?
Piercing deep into her eyes
I darted my gaze to throw some light.
And replied that I had good news.
But she intruded and said it could only be night.
Raising my brows I smirked but she was right.

In a manner somewhat new
blinking my eyes to show acute surprise.
I posed a question to her.
Had she really thought that I was caught
in her web of will so clever to disguise?
Drowning in tears never to stir.
Days are dull and nights are mysterious
I choose night for the reasons of spurious.

Love is to... Yearn for Sweet Dreams

Torn to pieces by the words he uses to scorn me.
For no reason, I am left to bear his wild screams.
And just to make him glad, I get busy like a bee.
Then he says love is to yearn for sweet dreams.

He is against sweet things in my life besides him.
And goes away whenever I want him on my side.
At times he plays games to be very bright or dim.
Surely he knows and thinks of me to be his bride.

He goes wild when I ask him to fulfil my needs.
A longing to love and be loved without any rage.
Changing ways and means, wishes with no leads.
There is no slumber of peace only a friendly cage.

So to make my life a bit easier and worth living.
I am all set and keen to share his sweet dreams.
Even when he admires and finds a song to sing
I break and he restores pieces of all my themes.

Vision of Politics

Myopia? An innate feature of politics I am made to face.
At best its vision drags up to five or even ten long years.
Able orator and egoistic people take all the main space.
Secular and free vision of politics without fright or fears.

Foresights of a chosen few make up for the way ahead.
And managed means are used to unite groups for gains.
Distinct words and slogans stand to create a watershed.
Thereby forming a rift among the various sects of brains.

At times manifesto lists an agenda of a secret pretence.
The two end views and the middle vision are set apart.
Pledge and promises starts to appear deep and dense.
And affairs of state aren't made to touch people's heart.

Partners in power or marriage of posts hands in the key.
But the doors are open to the viewers like swarm of bee.
Distinct or blurred the vision of politics is always marred.
Due to the feature of politics, from it entry or exit is hard.

A Man of Repute

He stood up to face the adversity
even when his love left him in pain.
Dare not rebuke instead he kept calm
for days and ends come sunshine or rain.
Then he had his future to think of
fortune or misfortune he must pay a tribute.
And as his long life lay ahead
in line with his standing as a man of repute.

Like a fairy tale the good times
in stages showed up page by page.
Scene after scene like day after night
a quick escape of memories from mind's cage.
The agony and shock of love lost
emerged to show as a forgotten dream.
Then only time and space remained to witness
outcome of this painful scheme.

Tainted for what was a mere mistake
on his part in carrying out his task.
Surely he took greatest of care
to reveal the truth taking off the mask.
Nothing left to chance and no stones unturned
in each and every aspect of his life.
With each heart beats all his regrets
reached out to show love to his wife.

Now more than ever he stands to guard
his firm faith in his rank and place.
Some give and take to make life bearable
he is willing to make but with grace.
Haunting past in no way is allowed to enter
into his peaceful and serene way of living.
Love is most welcome to reside in his heart
no doubt without any mistrust or misgiving.

The Difference Between...
Idle and Lazy

How to tell if some one is being just idle or lazy?
One must look for his or her gestures and display.
Willing but held up to act is the sign of being idle.
Whereas apathy makes him or her a lazy so to say.
But all in all the difference between idle and lazy
rests the way one does his or her deeds of the day.

When calm takes hold and willingness to act dies.
When values are of no use and conscience sleeps.
Then there is no change of opinion and or views
in the manner the acts or deeds bounces and leaps.
Though one is able to gauge the scope or the range
in the difference between idle and lazy for keeps.

Trick of the Trade

One needs to know the technique to perform well.
In other words it is known as the trick of the trade.

When it grows to be a habit it turns into a problem.
And skills gained pricks into life like a sharp blade.

Realize the state without the knack of doing things.
Chaotic world all around, no calm, shine or shade.

We ought to thank for the receptacle of know how.
To one and the only one who bestowed us this aid.

Necessity does not Wait

Bare necessity does not wait for the right time to come.
Like hunger or thirst never sees if food or drink is near.

Mostly found that needs arise at a worst possible time.
Pain for some but it is the way of the nature to adhere.

With or without an option it is faced with lack or ease.
But quite a few have the horn of plenty, cheap or dear.

While it is said that necessity is the mother of invention.
The well being of nations lies within the span far or near.

If in Doubt

A dilemma, hesitation or misgiving is a sure sign
leading to uncertain events to expose and shout.
Acts past or present do not show the best in line.
Hence examine the facts in the future if in doubt.

At times belief impedes the way to swift results
and surety decides how fast or slow to change.
End of an event means the dawning of the next.
While certainty builds, doubt stays out of range.

Depth of conviction is not a measure of desires.
It just shows roots of intent in terms of reliance.
Minimise what it means to be in a state of frenzy.
If not embark upon the floating ship of defiance.

To be brave and build a normal way of life to lead.
Awful though it may seem at times when in doubt.
Just go through the facts of the past one by one.
Rest at ease with the facts and figures with clout.

Double Your Trouble

Lovingly if your other half asks you for a night out.
You must drop all you have planned for that night.
Otherwise get ready to face a war of will and want.
Or double your trouble in lovely times or gallivant.

Any given reason is sure to create a cloud of grief.
Pour out no anger upon the feelings of other half.
Loving and care may drop like a fallen winter leaf.
Solitude may stretch like a long sketch or a graph.

Comfort is hard to catch for self-seeking reasons.
Even highly spirited souls need farsighted visions.
Hate is the other face of double sided coin of love.
Do not ignore any side left, right, below or above.

A little thought, little praise and real keen interest
lifts the level of love to a point of no return in time.
We truly take it for granted that all our other halves
are there to strike any notes for him or her to chime.

True Love

Feelings ablaze, unrest and unease of a kind
sleepless nights pitch black with dreamy days.
Heart beats racing to the moon, hoping to find
missing zest in life true love, in so many ways.

Lost in the maze of impulsive and futile search.
Actions have no past or future without an aim.
Count not grains of losses or gains out in lurch.
Things unknown in the future may achieve fame.

Pretence or ploy, love makes a mark on mind.
Heart remains safe but memories, they do last.
Over time result of love return to haunt or bind
eternal grief of hate tied to life's resilient mast.

Without a doubt pleasure is the gift of true love.
And love a blissful wealth of life to be enjoyed.
Never to lose heart if in trouble over and above
true love is a passion in itself not to be denied.

Nice to Talk

At times it makes sense to raise your voice.
For silence is the root of boom and blast.
Heightened tenacity can never be a choice.
If the words of solution is driven fast.
Sounds muted and words gagged
tongues tied to an endless string of rock.
After an ongoing and long lasting hush
it's so wonderful and nice to talk.

While peace of mind and stable heart beat
we all need for a good night's sleep.
Cry for a quiet moment and hungry to eat
no tone of voice to raise shallow or deep.
Born crying to make our presence known
and begin to talk in times of good or bad.
From turn to crawl and laughter to moan
we live our lives talking happy or sad.

Test for Love

How do I know that I am in love?
Affection, fondness, love and care.
Are all of these feelings fused as one?
Sunk in my heart; I must find out.
All about these strange effects.
And if there is a test for love?

Even so emptiness fills my heart.
But pain of being wanted goes on.
And I am unable to avoid my senses
being seized one by one.
Is this the proof or test for love?
When it's all said and done.

I go mad just thinking about love.
There is no affection or care in sight.
Hate is the real villain in conformity
of my acts and beliefs day and night.
Where foolish heart and wise mind
weaves the acts of accord or enmity.

Enough of bearing this longing and crave.
Truly I am not willing to wait
for a miracle to emerge and save.
So, I have devised a rule for test.
If it is love and not the charm
just wish me good luck and all the best.

Cruel to be Kind

If being nice causes to commit a crime.
It is right to take steps and find.
A caring way to deal with in good time.
Onc has to be cruel to be kind.

To display a callous and cruel nature
in itself may not result in good deeds.
Also true it is, nice and a good feature
will not grow just sowing tender seeds.

Opposing the phrase cruel to be kind
stands killer kindness just like a rock.
Other truism doesn't come to my mind
but it's more than enough to give a shock.

Cast of a good nature has to evolve
passing through the nasty and mean.
Cogs and wheels of charm to devolve
like a mirror of marvel nice and clean.

The Difference Between...
Struggle and Strife

Doing the best that can be done
on any day at any time.
Physical or mental there is no limit
no barrier, nothing left to chance
for the lack or abundance of cent or dime.
So the struggle goes on.

To bear the burden of discord
or fight to stay ahead of trial of life.
Clashes and conflicts slam the door
and contention ceases the will to live.
We seek to enhance our well being
and strive for more and more.

However we may try to separate the two.
But the difference between struggle and strife
remains delicately intertwined.
Through out the span of life.

Hard Headed Man

Some of us are distinct, firm and resolute
by shape, build, habit and nature.
There is no way to shift, change, move, ban
dismiss or discharge from their stature.
The only way to describe, depict or tell
their acts are to know them as hard headed man.

Problem arises when a change is in need
due to the change in nature.
But he is so stuck in his way of living
there is no room to move about or change.
Habits and habitat both are there to support
with no reason or cause for forgiving.

Distant he might be from the norm
of day-to-day dealings.
In his heart he knows and value
the people and thus react to their feelings.
So, with is outer hard skin, his inner softness
remains hidden out of the view.

A showman he may be for every one to see
but carries a real beating heart.
Feelings of hurt and at times agonising pain
bubbles up though he plays to be real smart.
Kindness touches him like a shock
and his hard headedness turns into a real art.

Laws of Emotion

First law of emotion aims to create feelings of the kind
which ignites a fire of longing in some ones chosen heart.
Second law states never let sentiments on the rise to find
anger and hate cut through trust or make believe set apart.
The third law of emotion sets up well-suited rules to bind
hearts and minds all together as one till death us do part.

How to deal with enraged feelings on the brink of disaster?
When the first law fails to catch longing within its sphere.
And when sentiment grows to be slave and not the master.
Doing what's right against all odds and no hope to adhere.
Last but not the least opposite rituals turns to react faster.
Heart breaks and mind blows with an awful cry of fear.

What if longing drowns in the pool of dislikes and disbelief?
And there is no exit from the storm of emotional ignorance.
A change in attitude like changing colour of a winter leaf
is not blamed for the rising level of anger and abhorrence.
The laws of emotion surely help when joy turns into grief.
Together or used alone it's sure to steal peace and tolerance.

Law is the saviour of heart and soul from aches and pains.
Even if obsession at times hinders our progress and wishes.
And awareness raises the flow of love and care in our veins.
And laws of emotion bind the craze and zeal that unleashes.
Passion is there to uplift and react with rising needs or gains.
Above all we're slave of laws with all their hits and misses.

Love...Expanse of Love

An incident today made me to retreat
when I was in my teens.
And I recalled friends raise a question
innocently with great unease.
It was somewhat a daunting task for me.
A challenge to answer in simple words
the most usual feelings of hearts and minds.
The question was what is love.
Decades later I am still trying my best
to seek the most apt reply.
My answers are under four headings
and here they are.
Physical and Platonic love stands to be the first.
Power and material wealth is next in line.
But most revered is Spiritual and Psychological love.
Last is the Love of Nature and Identity.

Love...Physical and Platonic

Parental love in the expanse of love is the most gracious and chaste.
Siblings are there to share affection with all delights and happiness.
Partners in our lives are a supreme gift of body with emotional mix.
Others like relatives; neighbours and friends are part of this feeling.

Disobedience works as a wedge between parents and their children.
Flame of jealousy begins to burn affection, love and care of siblings.
And imbalance between physical and platonic love devastates lives.
What remains may become a thing of the past never to be recalled.

There are those who believe love to be the work of vacuous intellect
to fill the gap between the activities of the valuable hours of the day.
At the other end love is taken as the soul of humanity without which
we are lost on the high way of life trying to find the reasons of living.

Sometimes it is tricky to control the upsurge or downturn of emotion.
Either way it creates mayhem of enormous extent leading to disaster.
This is the nature of love without which we are no more than a stone.
So be it physical or platonic we lead our lives as an ideal social being.

Love...Power and Material

Lavish land of love is also possessed and ruled by power
acquired by means of money, land and even sheer health.
Their need is power even if they have to gulp and devour
their own flesh and blood either knowingly or by stealth.

Tactical moves are made to find means as yet out of reach.
Where pride and self-interest takes lead over all other acts.
No options are left untouched without sucking like a leach.
The end may not be fruitful but the power has its impacts.

Man, money and material surely give an edge over the rest.
But in time mighty turns weak unable to stand on its own.
Then a realization creeps in about the inability of this zest.
He or she lives helpless and unloved not even able to moan.

So, for some money and power is love and love is power.
Power to rule, power to deal, power for the sake of control.
Power to fight and power to make innocent die by the hour.
There are no better weapons to separate body from the soul.

Love...Spiritual and Psychological

Enshrined with a mystical mind are human beings.
Allowed to form a basis of living with ease.
A serene heart to create a psychic faith.
And emotional flow to hide and save diverse views.
The beliefs that take shape in a varied form
creating devout of love and peace.

It's best to display the image of our thoughts.
But the way of life comes in between
beliefs, faith and creed standing at the side.
Mental zest seems to be at war
with emotional state of our hearts.
And love of life stays at ease till the worry departs.

The greatest recipient of our love is the faith we hold.
In a way it is the echo of our conscience.
Slaves of conformity and masters of our will
we are all keen to follow the order of the day.
May it be physical, spiritual or psychic events?
Our cry for love is relentless and forever.

Love...Local and Global

Reflection of emotional myopia is a narrow view of localism.
Where natives become obsessed with self-view of their origin.
A deep thought and an inquisitive glance at the natural world
ought to show diversity and global ways and means to coexist.
Love; by nature is a global phenomenon and should be for all.
No biological or geographical merit should define its expanse.

Home or abroad there is a welcoming heart but rather in pain.
Is there a way to redress this misery caused by a fellow being?
Local versus national and national against global creates a call.
To rise up and face the shock of the day when love die in vain.
Love of the natives, love of the global and love natural world.
Open your eyes with open heart and love universal you'll see.

Some Other Time

Some other time is the phrase to kill the needs.
To avoid or elude time and space for set deeds.
Acts to meet promise to deny or to create a row.
Unwilling to agree, what needs to be done now.

Shifting the beads of time only prolong sorrow.
The words right now has no push for tomorrow.
Awaiting acts are replaced by just a few words?
Actions denied in line with current craze of girds.

Do's and don'ts stand no chance for a choice.
And an urge to do now turns stronger in voice.
Promises break and concern changes its face.
There is no way to be realistic just to interlace.

So in line with the ethics a plan is fixed to evolve.
Choices made now are held in future to devolve.
Last but not the least the phrase is upheld by all.
There is no repay for any loss incurred to recall.

But I Hate Love

Do you love me?
Holding the steering wheel
she glanced at me and asked.
Like a slave she stopped the car
and entwined her gaze with mine.
I tuned up to her tone and replied.
Sorry my dearest pet
but I hate love in any form.
But I hate love that splits and divide.

Why do you say that?
Her foot on the break she stopped
with a casual smile and posed.
Alarmed with sudden stop
I glanced ahead at the red light and said.
I have learnt to keep myself safe
from this infectious feeling
and stop aches and pains spreading.

So, do I take it that you do not love me?
She asked with some sadness in her voice
and speeded up with a jerk to move ahead.
Love cannot grow in a heart
where feelings of emotion are blocked.
Turning away from her said.
I have accepted and now like the dogma
love to hate and hate to love.

So, where do I stand with you
in this journey of love and romance?
Love me, love me not from dusk to dawn
you stand by me at all times good and bad.
You do really make me very, very sad.
We have found our place and here we stop.
With a placid face he gave a distant look at her
and said it's not hate either but I hate love.

Easy to Say

A Herculean task set for a man of ordinary stature and means.
Without any idea of ability to perform or do is very easy to say.

Could it be that task setter is blinded by the rules of the tasks?
Ignorance isn't the only sword of failure for the set task to slay.

Oddity remains a trait to be admired when there is no way out.
Complexity is not always hard to be solved or to be kept at bay.

Revealed to be trouble free or declared to be difficult and hard.
The time and effort is the main contender and is there to stay.

Blink of Her Eyes

A shimmering round pair of deep blue crucible of sea
made to shine on her face like a pair of slivery moon.
They show the inner feelings of a thousand colours
and exude an aroma of love from mid night to noon.
Her steely gaze throws a bait to catch a longing heart
and a slow death he dies with every blink of her eyes.

A gift of nature bestowed upon her as a hypnotic tool
at times brings a storm of fury only to cause her harm.
However tranquil or tense those watchful eyes try to be
they do tangle and intertwine with a view to charm.
At its worst with a prolonged stare eyes create a rift
and infuse a series of thoughts in her mind to disarm.

Her eyes shining with flames of passion
to give a new lease of life to those sleepy souls.
The life long hunger of love has left them aloof
on the high way of life without controls.
But her radiant look still keeps touching the senses
all around her without any aspirations and goals.

Her admirers are there for her at every step of the way.
To uplift her soul, to make sense and feel.
Like her there is no other in this world
which makes the wounded heart to heal
with just one blink of her eyes.
And that's the prime boon of creation and blessed deal.

A Way of Life

When duty lends a hand to stop an unfair act.
When right seeks a chance to make a claim.
When there is no way out but to agree a pact.
That is the time a way of life changes its aim.

Rights and duties; they do go hand in hand.
What if right is claimed unduly for own gain?
And duty ignored like a mere one nightstand.
All strive to change the lifestyle goes in vain.

Means to manage the value and worth of life
on the scale of duty and right is set by deeds.
Habits and ways tend to form a path for strife
while survival is tainted by wishes and needs.

There is no getaway from what is to be done.
Daily life is a mixed bag of the beads of events.
Privilege is a weight on the back of every one.
A way of life lived with pleasures or torments.

No My Love

Innocence glows on your face and smile casts a charm.
It is not easy to ignore any of your desires good or bad.
You enact the roles for me to play, no problem no harm.
Fail to notice you at any time, no my love I must be mad.

Patience is getting scarce as the time slowly vanishes
in the past with a view to escape from your loving hold.
I resent that you want me to dance under your lashes
though I agree to act and play the role in hot and cold.

Like a bad dream I shake and think of the day we met.
Giving out free the warmth of your love like a rising sun.
But going through the rise and fall of the golden sunset.
Crawl on my knees even when it was all said and done.

Fun and games we loved, they are no longer amusing.
Inside or out we seem to be always against each other.
There isn't any room for praise any more only abusing.
Is this the resolve, no my love? Let's get back together.

A Helping Hand

Far away places or near to home.
Man made threat or nature's calamity.
At the brink of disaster
or within the jaws of fatality.
A cry that reaches the peaks of the hills,
deep in the sea and across the land.
From each and every corners of the world
beings of conscience flock to lend a helping hand.

Thoughts and beliefs that leads a person to give
his or her precious moments of life.
Selfless they must be or egoistically they live
to meet their own psychological needs.
Morally high and compelled by a duty of care
to aid and facilitate helping hands to give and take.
Fight with their conscience when the time is right
to hand over all they possess for their feeds.

For some reason if the help is not in need
and calamity turns into a tale of success and joy.
Would there still be a caring heart
ready to give a child in lament a toy?
The dilemma remains between noble cause
and egoistic needs of the helping hands.
Some may turn their heads away
others may decide to remain stuck to their stands.

However, helping hands are a boon
for those poor and needy souls in dire distress.
Awaiting to be rescued and saved
from the brink of disaster and death.
Looking through the victim's baffled eyes
helping hands may gain from this act of aid.
But victims are the final receiver of this gift of life
without which candle of love will surely fade.

Gratitude

Is it enough to say thank you to convey gratitude?
Or should there be certain actual actions on offer.
If so, what shall be the form of deeds or aptitude?
Gifts to win hearts and minds or submit the coffer.

What if thanks veil the feelings of just being nice?
And deeds show no momentous triumph or failure.
Does it make any difference if one gives an advice?
To express an honest opinion of good behaviour.

Crave of gratitude and praise needs a way to feed.
By usual offer of help and advice to people at large.
At times reward turns out quite impossible to heed.
And losses endured in life are so hard to discharge.

Still effect of gratitude in life is greater than charm.
Other obligations can be disposed of in some way.
To repay thanks quest of soul is in need with calm.
More than that a heart to heart talk gets in to play.

The Difference Between... Timid and Shy

To spot the difference if a person is timid or shy.
We must look at the manners and precise sense.
If some one is anxious or just set to say goodbye.
He or she is bashful or even a loner over the fence.
But the difference between timid and shy is true.
Timid is anxious where shy is quieter in view.

When a timid tries to act as daring and brave.
He or she faces the noise of chaos for sure.
And if silence clouds the face of a lucky slave.
No one waits to lift the veil of shyness to lure.

There is a chain of genes coiling over desire
to face bold and brash with this bodily feature.
Assertive and live stays away from tamed fire
being so quiet and devoted bashful creature.

Features of life to hold and bear daily routine
in times of happiness or even when it turns sad.
The difference between timid and shy is seen
faced with an opposite feature crying like mad.

Beyond My Imagination

Far beyond my imagination
there lies a world of intrigue.
Hidden away under the layer of feelings
where not even my inner eyes can see.
Playing those mystic tunes of faith
my heart beats with the rhythms of joy.
With the enigma of the unknown
my spirited mind seeks a key to unlock belief.

When my imagination seeks to invade reality
and finds no way to enter or leave.
I stand at a loss unable to bear the truth of life
born to live and living to die.
A harmony that causes conflict and discord
live to love and love to hate and revolt.
A few moments of joy in my mind's eye
where is that peace, there I ought to be.

Within the confines of my physical being
lay creative mind and logical thoughts.
Gestures to reveal and expressions to show
my eyes to talk and smile to greet.
There are so many ways to live my life
Though, I must choose a right way.
All in all as a devout and sincere soul
I am playing a whole host of directed roles.

With open heart I carefully undertake
to do the duties given to me.
Obey and follow the rules by true means
and never deter or hinder the words of peace.
Glimpses of the past or vision of the future
but the present is here to hold me to account.
All of this seems so amazing and far-fetched
truly and honestly beyond my imagination.

Achieving Aims

To find the right way of achieving aims
some embrace logical and rational means.
Others may find the way by trial and error.
But the goal is just one and the same.

What if the course of achieving aims changes?
Or trial and error gets nowhere.
The set path is beset with tactical errors
or there are no rules to organize and check.

Without analysis there is no way to know
the nature and the context of the aims.
To predict and prescribe the ways and means
of avoiding the wrong path leading to way.

Win or lose depends upon the road we choose
to lead our lives and achieve our aims.
Keep our eyes open and follow the rules
of living our lives the right way.

How to be Nice?

Be nice to me that's all I want from you.
She says when I ask her something to do.
It is quite true; I am never angry or rude.
Looking straight into her eyes
talking softly with a warm smile I ask.
Please! Could you just show me how to be nice?

By nature she is easy going from day to day.
Makes no fuss about matters of concern.
Doing her best wherever she can.
And I have never raised even a probing eye.
Then she comes up with this sort of comments.
I just don't know why? Just don't know why?

In her heart she must think I treat her rough.
What have I done or said that is so bad?
She has a habit of saying such things.
And cares not how much she is hurting me.
One way or other I must make her realize
to see all the signs I show for being nice.

Being reminded all the while to be nice
even when I know that I am good and kind.
Bit by bit I am being eaten up by this remark.
Every day when I face her a thought comes to mind.
She cannot be so thoughtless not to know
that I care for her the most in this selfish world.

Body and Soul

I am yours my love with my body and soul.
Don't leave me alone when I've given you all.
Sacred vows and promises we have made.
Joined together at the altar after serenade.

How quickly you have become a stranger?
The man I knew is no more living with me.
It's true at times I've laid your life in danger.
I didn't mean to hurt you it was never to be.

My sweet, I must stop you leaving this way.
Anchor of my love is quite strong to break.
Many times you've tried to keep me at bay.
If it is to be I am glad to bear this heartache.

The mirror hanging at the wall of tomorrow
has the same face I have always admired.
All you care to offer, I accept joy or sorrow.
No qualms, not even a bit of praise desired.

Love is to...Live in Hope

Sleepless nights and painful days to go through
without the face that I framed in my eyes.
I am just like a heart with no beat.
Without you how long can this soul of mine cope?
I am now losing my desire to exist
but I must, love is to live in hope.

Memories are here to raise a storm of feelings
only to inflame all my aches and pain.
Leaving behind pieces of scattered broken heart
never to heal or wander in memory lane.
Though, I am sure that some day somewhere
my past will meet my future again.

Live to die and love to hate those days and nights
when you embedded senses good and bad.
There could never even be a moment in my life
to change the gift of your love, happy or sad.
Truly not needed in happiest of times
but I was there crying for love good or bad.

How do I reconcile my feelings with your love?
When I know you are no longer with me.
Today or tomorrow I will have to accept that
you have gone and will never come back to me.
Though deep down somewhere in my heart
just about to grow a seed of hope I see.

To Save Money

Go to any length to save money.
Stand in the queue in the freezing cold.
Not just an hour or two
but the whole night.
Oh what a fright!
Endure the hardship of hunger
without any food or drink.
Watch the bulge of the tummy to shrink.
And why not?
It's the money that pushes the rich to the brink.

Keep an eye on the news.
And know state of the nations worldwide.
What they are up to?
And why they are going bonkers?
Correction!!! Why the bankers are going bonkers?
It is the interest making it interesting.
Money to make business earn profit.
Pay exorbitant salaries and bonuses
to high earner employees and their bosses.
Oh! What a tactfully aimed hits and misses?

Money is to savour?
What a crazy thing to say?
Just seek a geek to lose billions in a day.
Or even better find an exec worthy of millions
while the volcanic nation erupts in anger.
Young and old, man or a woman
sleeps under the blanket of stars.
Body shivers in winter with hunger and thirst
trying utmost to sleep without any outburst.
What a dreadful state of affairs to bear?

Invest money to learn and then earn money to eat.
Pack money in the pocket to bank.
Money runs the buses money flies the plane.
Money on the train and money at the ship that sank.
Is there a place where money is not in need?
What an enquiring thought indeed?
It is the reality of this modern economic age.
Money is needed at every little step that we take.
Some have to slog for every penny to earn.
That is why one should be wise to save money.

Down the Drain

I work hard to get myself noticed by others.
And gain life long goal to be a famous man.
All my efforts, ideas and respect for others
seems to have slowly gone down the drain.

Once in a while I take time to rest and enjoy.
That's when they ask me to slog and sweat.
My return is like a child's play thing or a toy.
In fury I'm like a fish out of water in the net.

Some take it easy doing the duty of the day.
And paid aptly though not worthy of the sum.
Others go unseen without a hitch so to say.
In the end worthy of praise they do become.

So find a key to the door of name and fame.
Now all my efforts revolve round this theme.
No avenues and no target left out of my aim.
No hard work in future will go down the drain.

There is a Way

Let there be and there was.
It is the root of all known and yet unknown creation.
This presents an endless string of mysteries
with vast number of questions and answers.
That is why scope of rationale suggests
wherever there is a problem.
Solution is somewhere just waiting to be found.
It is also true if a question can be raised.
Then there is a just and right answer
hidden in the maze of insight and wisdom.
Search for a right path that leads
to that point where there is a way.

Do not know what to do or what's the answer?
A host of problems to be solved
but there does not seem to be a way out.
Trying hard in the dark expanse of ignorance
to swim out of the river of muddle and chaos.
Be brave and just ask someone who knows
the ways and means and problems in hand.
The answer or solution can be found
without too much hassle or waste of time.
Such is the confusion of the state of mind.

Blinded by greed and or wealth of ignorance
causes the good deeds to perish.
Where lack of knowledge and belief
leads gradual moral decline.
Life's most precious features are overlooked
in the shady maze of immoral acts.
There cannot be a richness of moral sense
when deprived souls are trampled at length.

Come to senses in the light of knowledge
and seek the true reasoning and reasons to be.
Leaving behind those fruitless daily routines
that gives no peace of mind and harmony.
Rampantly going through the various stages in life
reaching to a point of no return.
When absolute aim is to achieve an eternal life
with never ending pleasure, heavenly bliss and luxury.

Futile Deeds

I ask myself why do we all have to work so hard.
To make living standard better for those at large.
May be we carry an agenda written on the card.
Plan futile deeds within hours of being in charge.

They say work is dignity so I am led to believe.
But it does not make life painless and complete.
Where do I put drive and prospect in this regard?
Wanted a matchmaker to be in the driving seat.

My pride is at risk no jobs to be found anywhere.
Factories, shops, offices and mills closing down.
Cuts all across the civil service even the armies.
Nothing left uncut not even the helms of crown.

So, should I stand on my two feet and be proud?
Well! I am trying my best to stand on my two feet.
But I cannot, I'm slowly being strung up by intent.
Debating in the house of fame by majority of seat.

Our Faith

It is confidence that keeps us on track.
Wherever we go, whatever we do
and no matter what we say.
Our mind checks ways and means
whereas hearts commit to act and play.
Social limits are there to guide us till the end.
And culture lays the scheme to carry on
within the bounds of our faith.

When our faith faces a weakened resolve
and we know not how to make our voices heard.
When forces beyond our control
lead us to tread a path full of chaotic events.
No matter how hard we strive to be absolved.
Past deeds return to haunt again and again.
There is no way out but the only one
living for peace, by the peace and of the peace.

In limited span of our lives within birth and death
seeded to develop faith of many forms and shapes.
At times it gains distrust, despair and disbelief.
Only to emerge as a loser but it's too late.
Reward or punishment in life hereafter is in our fate.
Abide by the rules of the chosen path
or bear the consequence for eternity.
That is the way it is and has to be.

Sobriety and honesty needs to be our aim in life.
If we have to excel facing doubts and fears.
Take steps beyond the confines of moral decline
and make our presence known to oblivious masses.
There is no reason to let the peace die
even before it has seen the face of communal relief.
Reliance and trust shall prevail inland and outside
if we abide by the rules within the bounds of our faith.

Turning Back

Once I have made up my mind.
I'll go without any catch or find.
Traumatic living is more than enough
in wild world of this kind.
From my boss even if I get the sack.
No reason to stay and no turning back.

No fuss, no clash and no fight to carry on.
Where there is no war of want for me to stay.
Merit or thanks is nowhere to be seen or heard
for the hard work I put in all night and day.
Regrets and concern for being of no use
I will bear it all without having anything to say.

At times I wish not to be so firm and sure.
It's like a bad dream coming true.
Untried and unproven remedy for cure.
No trace of any wrongdoing or any clue.
There is only one way to put it right.
Stay ahead of any imposition of might.

I stand to fight any unjust act or deed
anywhere, any time or any place.
It is a weak and timid act not to heed
or react to known threats face to face.
I affirm and uphold if there is a lack
of praise, there will be no turning back.

The Difference Between…
Sharp and Quick

Use of sharp and quick is not just a matter of choice.
It is also the context of phrase and the mode.
Sharp is used to mean objects pointed, jagged or barbed.
Also a sound, high-pitched, piercing or shrieks.
It shows abrupt, harsh and cunning nature of a being.
Or simply be an exact and clear sign or deal.
Quick on the other hand is an action taken in haste.
A brief and sudden surge is meant when it is said.
Implication is there just to add a vigour and weight.
In some respect sharp and quick means the same.
While there is a fine line that divides the use.
The difference between sharp and quick is here to stay.

Flight of Imagination

Flight of imagination is endless in time and space.
There are no navigational aids or routes to follow.
Thought on the other hand has set idea and place
under consideration, a plan of work solid or hollow.

Over worked or under duress mind says no more.
No flight of fancy and no rambling above the norm.
Plan, facts and figures are pushed out of the door.
Parts of all concern, may it be a business or home.

The lack of insight and level of wisdom is the limit.
How long one can see from the gifted mind's eye?
Concept is left in its place not to send or transmit
any kind of answer some how, head has to deny.

Wave of emotional flares only delays the changes
needed to get a foothold in the depths of feelings.
Wise reasoning takes care of blemishes of heart
not to pass the limits of thought in ones dealings.

Cause of My Pain

Don't you even want to look at me?
And you do really make me insane.
Away from his hypnotic gaze I replied.
I hate you and this is the cause of my pain.

I love him, yet he treats me like a…
Well! You know what I mean.
I can see lust in his eyes.
But no trace of love I have seen.

I ought to give him the same cure.
To get him out of his agony.
Yet I rely upon his help for sure.
Just can't erase him from my memory.

I will have to live with his uncaring ways.
With broken heart and tears in my eyes.
Knows my love for him all nights and days.
He deceives and betrays me but denies.

Dark Days and Colourful Nights

Are there dark days and colourful nights?
If there are then what does it mean?
Think of the setting of a dull and boring day.
Or a night, playful and happy full of fun.
Well then it's just begun.
Getting to work at half past eight.
And mind you it's never too late.
Sitting by the fellow worker in assembly line.
Tea break, lunch and the day trails like vine.
Getting home by car, bus or bike.
Supper to taste and leaving for love to nightclub.
Dancing cheek-to-cheek or a new shoulder to rub.
A pint or two but never get involve in fights.
This we call dark days and colourful nights.

Like a...

Space! Like the blue sky or the heavens above.
Tiny! Like a grain of sand or a speck of dust.
Mean! Like a wealthy miser or a poor magpie.
Kind! Like a revered saint or mother of a child.
True! Like a heavenly word or a matter of fact.
Loving! Like a baby born or an act of worship.
Jealous! Like a lover highhanded or just selfish.
Warm! Like a hearty friend or an ally in need.

Blue sky is an illusion and heavens I think not.
Sand is tiny but fast wind creates a sand storm.
Wealthy miser is more liberal than a poor man.
A saint becomes aloof to share his kind nature.
Devine is always pure but facts can be tainted.
A baby is real whereas worship can be a show.
A lover fearful of losing trust in his or her love.
Closeness is not always a sign of friendliness.

Usually rains when sky turns cloudy and black.
A giant is wide open to face calamity of nature.
Generous people are more likely to be abused.
One doesn't always have to be cruel to be kind.
False perishes when faced with the real events.
Loathing is a sign of extreme emotional distress.
Pleasant persons are more likely to be trusted.
To be aloof and lonely is a sign of being unloved.

It is hard to find a breathing space in hectic life.
Even a tiny error can create a chain of mishaps.
Not to mean to cause harm is never an excuse.
Some of us are naturally kind to people in need.
To live life in true sense of human spirit is a joy.
Loving is never a painless and easy task to bear.
When acts are lacking jealous wishes spill out.
Alas only a few of us are born with warm nature.

Colours of Deceit

Colours of deceit like the seven colours of the rainbow
seems to be overlapped and go beyond quiet and calm.
The root of deceit is lying that holds all above and below
the steps of fraud, guile, fixing, sting, trickery and sham.

Fraud shows its streak linked with guile and other acts.
And fixing unites the sting operation to make a success.
Trickery at times becomes obvious to make any impact.
Sham on the other hand is so passive it ends in a mess.

Honesty is there to hold the progress of deceit on its trail.
No matter how far and wide the range of this evil may be.
Truth and reality weighs up the impact of deceptive scale.
And no avenues left unseen and no doors without a key.

Let there be a decisive change in moral code of conduct.
Allowing deceit and its shades on a route to self-destruct.
So as to reward openness and honesty in all walks of life.
Hail the true face of humanity with a new phase of strife.

The Difference Between... Doubt and Disbelief

What creates doubt and how it affects our resolve?
The main cause is the vague activities and deeds.
Disbelief is a feeling rising from all corners of heart.
It is the warning that keeps us away from reliance.
Or likely pitfalls of morally unfair ways and means.
Facing the difference between doubt and disbelief.

At times doubt moves the criteria of judgment afar
when behaviour or act seems quite untrue to rely.
And disbelief plays its part to put fair things away.
Only to confirm how we feel at the end of the day.

But certainty and poise stands to guard the dawn
from where doubt and disbelief begins to emerge.
There is no compromise and no arms to lay down
when belief takes control of conscience and soul.

However doubt and disbelief is like body and soul.
One without the other has not any chance to exist.
It is something opposite to ones ethics and belief.
Rather hard to erase from memory or conscience.

War of Wisdom

War of wisdom takes place when viewpoints clash
and difference in belief gets to a peak of no return.
Discord and conflicts rise to a level ready to slash
peace and harmony that has taken an era to earn.

Worlds apart they are but their ways are the same.
Ought to find a means to match their sincere aims.
Often it is hard to put a barrier to lower their fame.
Just a way to reduce the gap between their claims.

Peace and calm even at a cost of personal repute.
A preferred option on offer to the people as a rule.
No matter how foolish it may come out as a tribute.
The upheaval of wits will no longer exist as a tool.

Since Adam war of wisdom have been on the rise.
And facet to live in peace is on the slope of decay.
But it also enables he or she to win the noble prize.
So fight a war of peace but not only for act or play.

Who wants to Know?

A knock at the door may bring good news or bad.
Or news laden with emotion to react fast or slow.
Till now a face never came across happy or sad.
Look at the caller and pose, who wants to know?

Rules are there to obey when meeting a stranger.
Intended or by chance a term of contact be made.
Friendly and known makes it a guard or a keeper.
Practice and know how is a key to gain accolade.

Look for a clue and get an idea with a prying eye.
Something likes a big smile or a smirk on the face.
Even a solemnity, straight look or just a quick hi.
Leaves a mark upon inner feelings, as is the case.

The way to a friendship or just for a social contact
stay hidden in the tone and the words being used.
At the door or on the stage of life, a time to attract
or keep at bay the issues informative or confused.

Love is…To Help Someone in Need

How often to reach and what shall we call?
This generosity and a will of want to heed.
Stranger or dear he or she may seem to be.
Yes love; love is to help someone in need.

What if this notion never crosses our mind?
And we wait and watch till the time is right
for a cry of help to touch our sleepy hearts.
Still filled with zest and zeal cagey to fight.

Close to hearts or even far from our sights.
There is a barrier, which impedes our way.
While we're busy in work days and nights.
And at times self-interest comes into play.

Search our souls and truly give all we can
without seeking any gains or loss of a kind.
Turn into a trait borrowed or lent by genes
to make us slaves of inherent urge to bind.

People Who Believe

People who believe in fortune-teller or the star signs
lack conviction or have no aim in life.
They show their basic needs not met and unfulfilled
their desires and wishes full of strife.
It is simply their belief and not a commonly held view
to be naive from the aims of highlife.

Agreed with no proof just like an image in the mirror
facing a dilemma of no fixed shape.
A myth prolonged to become a ritual of the ages
tied to string of time unable to escape.

Disbelievers on the other hand face trials in daily life
at every step of the way in each effort.
And with no doubt they meet challenges with set aims
waving the flag of trust as their mascot.

Although at risk and unsure in their acts and deals
they tend to be guarded by their faith.
Wisdom lay at their feet but does not heed any caution
not to crawl back even as a wraith.

Behind Closed Doors

Fate of millions are either made or destroyed
in all places in every way with or without force.
Tradition plays its role to establish an accord
by majority count of vote behind closed doors.

None but one has the power to defy set rules
and change against the interest of public gain.
Since his plan creates, sets up and ridicules
rivals in line with the public needs to maintain.

How often and for how long he can carry on?
Time is not the only factor beyond his control.
There is an oceanic heads waiting just out
fighting to enter an arena to play political role.

Behind closed door but with their minds open
play politics with the fate of public at large.
What will happen decades later they know not?
By then they wouldn't be there to be in charge.

Wish Me Good Luck

A melodious voice that echoed in my ears.
All hours of the day without any gloom or fears.
Now seems to have slowly faded away.
Eager to join the lost souls on the Milky Way.
I wish if I could raise my arms and pluck
the strings of her voice to say wish me good luck.

I want to get ahead in my life without her.
But she lives in each and every beat of my heart.
I try hard to get her out without any upset or stir.
And find a way out or let her memory to impart.
Must find a means to forget and start my life afresh.
The way to find good luck is to get out of this mesh.

Peace by Demise

How to bring peace amidst conflict and chaos?
There has to be a way beyond the use of guns.
Fighting for peace in itself is an opposite ethos.
Peace by demise and death of our own sons!

An army to enforce a dialogue on the one hand.
On the other, millions are made to starve at will.
There is no just basis to create a nomad's land.
Where proceeds of thousand years are now nil.

To wage war without valid reason is just crazy.
Mainly when it is in the interest of the invaders.
Peace takes years to create, which is not easy.
All gains vanish like mist in front of the raiders.

Still, war goes on even if innocents die in vain.
And humanity acts to be like a blind and deaf.
The nation after nation stands at ease in pain.
Holding the dish of peace like a five star chef.

A Day to Remember

Thinking about a day to remember.
Not quite sure which one should come first.
The day I was born or the day I stood up.
Or the day when I took first momentous step.
Not to forget the first utterance of word like Mum?
My first bewildering day at the nursery
left alone with the strangers to play.
From all the first days that I can recall
the day of my first kiss when I fell in love.
Remains fresh like an early morning summer breeze
just above the horizon the rise of the golden sun.
A day to remember is the sight of just one loving face.

I am at a loss unable to pick and choose.
All of my first days are precious to me.
Could I possibly be without any one of those?
Who I am and how I stand back to appraise?
At times it's better to forget those days.
Ones that began with a joy only to end in tears.
Just like the end of the days lies the dark nights.
End of memory is not to recall and forget it all.
Even so at the end of a busy day.
It is nice to go back to those forgotten past.
And rejoice all of those events that gave us joy.
With the greatest of passion for love and life.

Take it All Back

Slandering or slur may be a habitual act
or an act of ignorance in the absence of fact.
Whoever defames without a glance at its source?
He or she is sure to regret in due course.

Failings and drawbacks are the result of trial indeed.
Showing the avenues and imprints of all efforts.
Innocence at times shrouds the tarnished image.
Only to expose the true nature of a being.

To seek solace from the ensuing misery and pain
is in the nature of a courageous man or a woman.
Thus do not shy away from this precious gift of nature
if a wrongful act or a word of slander has been done.

Last Resort

When a plan of action gets to a point
and seems not to achieve the desired result.
That's when a drastic step needs to be taken
in the last resort to rescue the ship of event.

Close contacts must be willing to help
and assist according to the needs of the day.
Inaction or an oversight could be the reason
for the mayhem, troubles and disarray.

In distress, out of touch and no way out.
Is there any point just to carry on till the last?
Let it be known to those who affirm to strive.
The end result is always linked to the past.

What comes next depends what's just gone?
And options are there for us to seek out.
Good or bad we must filter it through
the funnel of last resort without any doubt.

Gift of a Kind

A get well card, a bunch of flowers
or even a few words to greet.
Lying in bed with excruciating pain
someone has taken trouble to meet.
Try to sit up with a made up smile
helping hand of the nurse tries to find
a pillow or something to rest my back.
Grateful I feel with this gift of a kind.

It is very thoughtful of the visiting guests.
But they tend to forget the key facts.
It is the hospital bed and there is a limit
to how long I can sit.
Besides this the morning and evening
there is a fixed hours for visit.

Why is it that all goodness
hidden in the people that I know?
Comes to a boil, which I cannot enjoy.
While I am health wise feeling low.
Have I become such an infirm?
Not even willing to accept gift of a kind.

I must confirm that I am not being vain
on the contrary I want to say.
If all my relatives, friends
and the people I happen to know.
They showed me the same kindness,
concern, love and affection.
I will give all my gift of love to them
in return for their gift of a kind.

Make no Haste

Rushing around to get the job done lacks prudence.
And more often than not it results in terrible waste.
A key feature of the work done well is the patience.
Therefore, strive to take it easy and make no haste.

What if time limits the efforts in reaching the goal?
Or the pace of conduct is marred with clever intent.
One way or the other speed of action taken by all.
Controls the shape, size and spread of its content.

The motto of do or die runs in the slow lane of life.
To show the exuberance of patience is here to stay.
And swiftness has no sharp edge to slash like knife.
Though snail pace is out of order and kept at a bay.

When speed becomes the essence of living to win.
Even at a cost of precious moments just passing by.
A thought never occurs to make us turn and spin
that at the end all these activities will lead us to die.

Won't be Coming Back

Quietly he walked out from the arms of love.
No good bye, no tears and not even a sigh.
All he left was painful memories of the past.
And a note saying he won't be coming back.

He played a game of deceit and defiance.
At times candid but often a secret and obscure.
I always gave open heartedly all I had.
And warned not to go beyond the limit of vow.

I couldn't bear all his out of the way wishes.
And switched my tender loving for hate.
I didn't succeed in erasing the memories of past.
Not an easy task for all those years of being in love.

He was unaware that I had already made up my mind.
Not to carry on holding my breath for so long.
Now I believe miracles do take place like lightning.
I was left all alone but now I am ready to live again.

The Difference Between... Similar and the Same

On the face of it these two words
similar and the same seems to be alike.
But there is a fine distinction between them
according to their usage and the scene.
Similar indicates the nature of comparison
or identical in shape and size.
Whereas the word same signifies the equality,
matching or unchanged features.

The problem arises when these words are used
in place of each other with no qualms.
Raising a an eye brow is the result
if and when it's all taken in.
Like when describing a well-known face
to a friend by saying he or she looks similar.

It is wise to bear in mind the situation
before the choice of word is made.
How different or alike is the scene on hand?
Looking at the objects of expression as a whole.

So, just to settle the argument
lets come to a common term.
When it's comparable or identical in all aspects
use of the word similar is in need.
And when it's equal, matching and or unchanged
of course on the word same we'll have to heed.

Pretence of Care

I am deeply disturbed by her pretence of care.
Leading me to stray out of her beguiling hold.
Love I can't give and the pain is hard to bear.
She tries to buy love though it's already sold.

A show of love is obvious the way she looks.
I follow her every move with a keen interest.
She stays one step ahead of me just to oblige.
And I am unable to chase her or keep abreast.

She must live by the rules of honesty in love.
And I mustn't alienate her by a show of hate.
Reunion of thoughts we both should create.
No breach of trust and no more futile debate.

Honesty in love is the key to pleasure and joy.
So I guess she knows what she stands to gain.
Pretence or real she has to make a good choice.
Love keeps me humble and hate makes me vain.

Horizon of Needs

When a torrent of idea strikes at the brim of imagination.
And hunger of thought craves for a will to do.
Spark of invention lights up the spaces of brain.
Welcoming heart takes a step into a world of future.
For all to feel and see the advantages and its use.
Something new is rising from the horizon of needs.

An eye of suspicion opens the door of neglect.
For all to watch the play of back and forth.
There is all praise and appreciation in one quarter.
And on the other side of the wall lies scorn and slate.
But the time plays its part to make up the difference.
New and fresh is sure to emerge from the past in the future.

Tears

The world turns upside down
when love changes its face.
The face that radiates sweetest of smiles
now glows with anger and hate.
It is the love that draws
inside out never, never to let go.
And hate keeps miles and miles apart
only to shed tears to come close.

Like the two sides of an emotional coin
side of love has the strongest of lure.
The other side is embedded with
anguish, pain, distrust, dislike and hate.
Living on the sea-saw of night and day
becomes a burden of immense weight.
A point in time decides to make or break
the string of life so lovingly carried thus far.

Love like the full moon showers its magic
to cage in a loving heart unable to leave.
Whereas black cloud of hate engulfs
all desires and wishes never to come close.
One way or other two hearts but one soul
turns into a trauma with no cure.
Love and hate running side by side
knowing not when and where to unite or go.

So let there be no quarrel of any shape or size.
And no gap between the two faces of hearts.
Yell and scream of hate or melodious echo of love
like a body and soul is just one.
The state of limbo or half way house
knowing not which way to go.
By nature opposites exist in the rules of creation
like the beginning and the end.

Politicians

Pleasing manners and point of views to match.
Of the cuff solutions for the people of the nations.
Linguists and speakers to spread the views to the masses.
Ideally open hearted but unwilling to accept a change.
Take it or leave it is the acquired attitude they use.
Ingenious though one-track mind and borrowed thoughts.
Collaborates with the policies for self-gain and security.
Image is a feature for him or her to maintain at all cost.
Admiration is used as bate to win hearts and minds.
Nationalism and nepotism is their second nature.
Socially soft and polite but tough with all alien scenes.

A Hidden Desire

We all cling to a hidden desire to be at the top in our hearts.
From the first step we strive to gain a foothold by all means.

Limelight of life is enough to make us stray from this path.
Besides, we certainly lose the urge to succeed in this regard.

Often to excel in our lives we slide down to a drain of defeat.
Never to raise our heads to revive hidden wishes in our hearts.

It is best not to know the hidden desires bestowed upon us.
To excel is in our hands if we focus our acts to meet the goal.

The Difference Between... Fate and Destiny

Fate and destiny! Are they really the same?
On the face of it, they may seem alike.
But if one dives deep into its core and context.
The difference between fate and destiny is clearly seen.
Fate is the result of all efforts and deeds.
And destiny? It is the place of result yet to come.

Some of us without any efforts and deeds
curse the result to be their fate.
Others consider destiny to be the blind faith
with no regard of time and place.

A claim of action is not enough to make way.
Or reserve a good or bad deed.
Just as knowledge on its own is of no use.
Till applied at a place of need.

So try harder to get the result we seek.
Instead of laying the blame on fate.
There is no better way to find our destiny
and strive to reach the last and final place.

Just Wait and Watch

She ventured out of step and beyond the limits of reasoning.
No regret, no touching gestures and not even a loving word.
Dreadful thoughts cross my mind about her thoughtless run.
I'll have to just wait and watch with all my vigour and zeal.

Love is all I could give no opulence, not even a place to live.
But she says love alone doesn't make her feel good and well.
I can see her needs of every day living enlarge like a balloon.
There is no way I can satisfy all her rising demand of needs.

Given the position I find myself in I ought to keep my wits.
And let the time take its course along the chosen path of will.
My neglect might lead her to the way of interest and intrigue.
In the future to cross each other's path very much like a fiend.

So, how to measure love on the scale of money and wealth?
Physical wants most of the time outweigh the psychic needs.
Flesh and bones do need to be fed by the earnings of money.
I'll have to be patient and satisfied by the lost sweet honey.

Stand to Win

To represent and be the voice of the people.
These days you've to learn ways and means of manipulation.
Then acquire the tongue that's never too sweet or sour.
Just the right tone of speech shall stand to win.

Like a note out of tune sounds to be odd.
Dual acts are damned and sure to fail in its aim.
Life in the common view must mimic and act the same.
There is no place for two in one act in public domain.

Stand away from the call of people and lose your support.
Walk out like a nomad from the polling booths.
Sit close to a few admirers hand in hand.
Hoping to stand again in near future.

There is a hidden storm of change within muted mass.
Just like a volcano it only erupts when it is ignored.
A wise mind with a good heart always heeds.
When the only aim in life is to stand to win.

Promises…

Spur of the moment assertions are made to assure.
No thoughts given about the situation yet to come.
Plight and pain is ignored on account of good luck.
For now affairs are safe as the promises are made.

Forces out of control when strikes all of a sudden.
There is no defence but agreeing to the end result.
Promise now broken tends to reveal its true worth.
And promisor stands to lose life long earned trust.

Then there are those who wouldn't make promise.
Come what may is their view towards life's event.
By nature they are prone to easy come and easy go.
Even if they have to bear and endure night and day.

So, promise only if the result is within your reach.
No show of charm or clout can save the bleak day.
When you've to face the reality of broken promise.
Facing the open world of bemused friends and foe.

Lightning Source UK Ltd.
Milton Keynes UK
UKOW02f0735140317
296535UK00001B/45/P

9 781630 043025